W9-BCN-053

FAVORITE PRAYERS
FOR CHILDREN

Nihil Obstat: Reverend Michael L. Diskin, Assistant Chancellor
Imprimatur: Most Reverend Thomas J. Olmsted, Bishop of Phoenix
Date: July 9, 2014

By Bart Tesoriero
Illustrated by Miguel D. Lopez

catholic
children's
CLASSICS

ISBN 978-1-61796-143-4

Our Father

Our Father, who art in heaven,

hallowed be Thy name.

Thy kingdom come,

Thy will be done, on earth as it is in heaven.

Give us this day our daily bread;

and forgive us our trespasses,

as we forgive those who trespass against us;

and lead us not into temptation,

but deliver us from evil.

Amen.

Hail Mary

Hail Mary, full of grace,

the Lord is with thee.

Blessed art thou among women,

and blessed is the fruit of thy womb, Jesus.

Holy Mary, Mother of God,

pray for us sinners,

now and at the hour of our death.

Amen.

Glory Be

Glory be to the Father,

and to the Son,

and to the Holy Spirit,

as it was in the beginning,

is now, and ever shall be,

world without end.

Amen.

Daily Offering to the Sacred Heart of Jesus

For love of me You came to earth;

You gave your life for me.

So every day You give me now

I give back happily.

Take all my laughter, all my tears,

Each thought, each word, each deed,

And let them be my all-day prayer

To help all those in need.

My Daily Consecration to Mary

O Mary, my Queen and my Mother,

I give myself entirely to you.

And as proof of my devotion,

I consecrate to you this day

my eyes, my ears, my mouth, my heart,

my whole being, all for you!

O good Mother,

As I am your own,

Keep me and guard me

As your property and possession.

Amen.

Come Holy Spirit

Come, Holy Spirit,

fill the hearts of Your faithful,

and kindle in us the fire of Your divine Love.

Send forth Your Spirit

and we shall be created,

and You shall renew the face of the earth.

Let us pray:

O God, who by the light of Your Holy Spirit,

has instructed the hearts of Your faithful,

grant us by the same Spirit to be truly wise

and ever to rejoice in His consolation,

through the same Christ our Lord.

Amen.

Prayer to My Guardian Angel

O Angel of God,

my Guardian dear,

To whom God's love,

commits me here;

Ever this day,

be at my side,

To light and guard,

to rule and guide.

Amen.

Prayer to
Saint Michael

Saint Michael the Archangel,

defend us in battle.

Be our protection against the wickedness

and snares of the devil.

May God rebuke him, we humbly pray;

and do thou, O Prince of the heavenly host,

by the power of God,

cast into hell Satan and all the evil spirits,

who wander through the world

seeking the ruin of souls.

Amen.

Act of Contrition

(Rite of Penance)

My God,

I am sorry for my sins with all my heart.

In choosing to do wrong

and failing to do good,

I have sinned against You

whom I should love above all things.

I firmly intend, with Your help,

to do penance,

to sin no more,

and to avoid whatever leads me to sin.

Our Savior Jesus Christ

suffered and died for us.

In His name, my God, have mercy. Amen.

The Memorare

Remember, O most gracious Virgin Mary,
that never was it known,
that anyone who fled to thy protection,
implored thy help,
or sought thy intercession,
was left unaided.

Inspired by this confidence,
I fly unto thee,
O Virgin of virgins my Mother.
To thee do I come, before thee I stand,
sinful and sorrowful.
O Mother of the Word Incarnate,
despise not my petitions,
but in thy mercy hear and answer me.
Amen.

Grace Before Meals

Bless us, O Lord,

and these Thy gifts,

which we are about to receive

from Thy bounty,

through Christ our Lord.

Amen.

Grace After Meals

We give You thanks, O Lord,

for these and all Thy blessings,

which we have received

from Thy bounty,

through Christ our Lord.

Amen.

Psalm 23

The Lord is my shepherd;
I shall not want.

He makes me to lie down in green pastures;
He leads me beside the still waters.
He restores my soul.
He leads me in the paths of righteousness
for His name's sake.

Yea, though I walk through the valley
of the shadow of death,
I will fear no evil,
for You are with me.
Your rod and Your staff,
They comfort me.

You prepare a table before me
in the presence of my enemies.
You anoint my forehead with oil,
and my cup overflows.

Surely goodness and mercy shall follow me
all the days of my life;
and I will dwell in the house of the Lord forever.

The Angelus

The Angel of the Lord declared unto Mary.
And she conceived by the Holy Spirit.
(Hail Mary...)

Behold the handmaid of the Lord.
Be it done unto me according to thy word.
(Hail Mary...)

And the Word was made Flesh.
And dwelt among us.
(Hail Mary...)

Pray for us, O Holy Mother of God.
That we may be made worthy of the promises
of Christ.

Let us pray:

Pour forth, we beseech Thee, O Lord,
Thy grace into our hearts; that we to whom
the Incarnation of Christ, Thy Son,
was made known by the message of an Angel,
may by His Passion and Cross,
be brought to the glory of His Resurrection.
Through the same Christ our Lord. Amen.

Prayer of Saint Francis

Lord,
Make me an instrument of Your peace.
Where there is hatred, let me sow love.
Where there is injury, pardon;
Where there is doubt, faith;
Where there is despair, hope;
Where there is darkness, light;
And where there is sadness, joy.

O Divine Master,
grant that I may not so much seek
To be consoled, as to console;
To be understood, as to understand;
To be loved, as to love;
For it is in giving that we receive;
It is in pardoning that we are pardoned;
And it is in dying that we are born to
eternal life.
Amen.

Bedtime Prayer

Now I lay me down to sleep,

I pray the Lord my soul to keep:

May God guard me through the night,

And wake me with the morning light.

Amen.

Family Prayer

God made us a family. We need one another.
We love one another. We forgive one another.
We work together. We play together.
We worship together.
Together we learn God's Word. Together we grow in Christ.
Together we love all people. Together we serve our God.
Together we hope for Heaven. These are our hopes.
Help us obtain them, Father, through Jesus your Son,
Our Lord. Amen.